Ziggurat

PHOENIX POETS

PETER BALAKIAN

Ziggurat

THE UNIVERSITY OF CHICAGO PRESS
Chicago & London

The University of Chicago Press, Chicago 60637
The University of Chicago Press, Ltd., London
© 2010 by The University of Chicago
All rights reserved. Published 2010
Paperback edition 2011
Printed in the United States of America

20 19 18 17 16 15 14 13 12 11   2 3 4 5 6

ISBN-13: 978-0-226-03564-2 (cloth)
ISBN-13: 978-0-226-03566-6 (paper)
ISBN-10: 0-226-03564-6 (cloth)
ISBN-10: 0-226-03566-2 (paper)

Library of Congress Cataloging-in-Publication Data
Balakian, Peter, 1951–
    Ziggurat / Peter Balakian.
        p. cm. — (Phoenix poets)
    Poems.
    Includes bibliographical references.
    ISBN-13: 978-0-226-03564-2 (alk. paper)
    ISBN-10: 0-226-03564-6 (alk. paper)
    I. Title. II. Series: Phoenix poets.
    PS3552.A443Z35 2010
    811'.54—dc22   2009052686

♾ This paper meets the requirements of ANSI/NISO
Z39.48-1992 (Permanence of Paper).

for ED HARRIS

CONTENTS

ACKNOWLEDGMENTS

My grateful acknowledgments to the editors of the magazines in which these poems, sometimes with different titles, first appeared:

AGNI: sections 1–33 and 42–43 of "A-Train / Ziggurat / Elegy"
Ararat: "Early Spring"
Boston Review: "Warhol / Blue Jackie"
Colorado Review: "Three Decades"
The Harvard Review: "Warhol / Electric Chair / '63"
Meridian: "Self-Portrait With Bird," and "The Alley"
New Letters: "Reading Dickinson / Summer '68," and "Blue Room"
Slate: "Going to Zero," "Blue" (section 38 of "A-Train / Ziggurat / Elegy")
Virginia Quarterly Review: "World Trade Center / Mail Runner / '71," "World Trade Center / Mail Runner / '73," "World Trade Center / Black Holes / '74," "Sarajevo"
"Warhol / Madison Ave. / 9-11" was published in a limited edition broadside by Arrowsmith Press, Cambridge, MA (April 2007).
"Warhol / Electric Chair / '63" was broadcast on *Poetica*, ABC Radio National, Australia (September 2008).
"World Trade Center / Mail Runner / '71," "World Trade Center / Mail Runner / '73," and "World Trade Center / Black Holes / '74" received the 2007 Emily Clark Balch Prize from the *Virginia Quarterly Review*.

Much gratitude to Bruce Smith, Bruce Berlind, Jennifer Brice, Doris V. Cross, Donna Frieze, Walter Kalaidjian, Helen Kebabian, Denise Leone, Matt Leone, Robert Jay and BJ Lifton and the Wellfleet Meetings, Askold Melnczyuk, Robert Pinsky, Tom Sleigh, Eric Simonoff, Chuck Strozier, Chris Tilghman, and Jack Wheatcroft. Immense gratitude to Yaddo.

One

GOING TO ZERO

I.

A canvas with less turpentine, more hard edges, less bleeding,
that was good for beauty, Frankenthaler in *Art News*

in the dining car crammed with parkas and laptops
micro-waved cellophane, plastic plates and canvas bags,

and the valley under fog as the cows disappeared
and when the green came back into view I could see

the SUVs floating on the Thruway, the cows oblivious
to the revved engines of trucks. The river glistened

all the way to Albany, and I could see flags on Baptist churches
and resurrection trailers, "God Bless America" on pick-ups—

"United We Stand" laminated to billboards
as the fog settled then lifted, and when I woke

a flag the size of a football field hung from the gray tower of the GW,
where the tractor-trailers jammed beneath its hem

as something sifted down on the silver-plated Hudson.
And then the lights went out.

2.

The faces on 7th Avenue blurred in the chaos of vendors and liberty
scarves, freedom ties, glowing plastic torches, dollars and polyester—

and inside Macy's I was hit by cool air as "Stars and Stripes Forever"
floated down from women's fashions into the quiet aisles of Aramis and silk
     scarves.

I wanted to buy the Frankenthaler, a modest, early print,
minimal, monochromatic; surface and perspective in dialogue;
on 24th off 10th—the gallery still smelled like wood and plaster—

but I didn't stop, and when the train reached the Stock Exchange
the Yom Kippur streets were quiet, and the bronze statue of Washington
was camouflaged by national guard. I was walking my old mail route now

like a drunk knocking into people, almost hit by a cab
until the roped-off streets cut me at the arm. At Broadway and Liberty
the fences wound around the bursts of dust rising

over the cranes and bulldozers, over the punched-out windows—
I stared through a piece of rusted grid that stood like a gate to the crystal
     river.
I was sweating in my sweatshirt now, the hood filling with soot,

as I watched with others drinking Cokes and eating their pizza of disbelief.
Zero began with the Sumerians who made circles with hollow reeds
in wet clay and baked them for posterity.

At Broadway and Liberty. At 20 floors charred and standing.
At miasma people weeping. Anna's Nail Salon, Daikichi Sushi,
the vacant shops, stripped clean in the graffiti of dust-coated windows.

Something blasted from a boom box in a music store,
something, in the ineffable clips of light,
disappeared over the river.

WARHOL / MADISON AVE. / 9-11

When I left Eli Zabar the cut-out star on the window
was whirling in the animation of the rich and hungry
hunched over tables for a $30 sandwich and a Diet Coke.

It was raining and the blurred glass of the galleries
was the gold leaf of the Carrig Rhone frames—
Childe Hassam's dabs of Connecticut trees

the diaphanous blue on the fleshy rocks,
the melting opal of the shoals.
Inside the Whitney the rain trailed down my face;

and I found myself in a quiet corner staring
at the pink face of Marilyn Monroe.
I could still smell the smoldering high-tech plastic

as it burned the air. In the whiteness of her teeth,
in the almost aahh of her mouth and the half-drugged eyes
under the lids of teal shadow, the air kept singeing my nose.

Against the pale walls Marilyn's face dissolved
like the stretched mesh and litho ink
where plain form is a place of no desire

like the empty mirror of the Hudson at dawn.
In the fissures of her make-up, the planes of color
led back and back behind her teeth longing—

to the deception by the Falls on her honeymoon
(with Joseph Cotton in *Niagara*)—where we found her clothed
and alarmed, and later desperate for the affirmation,

of a President's limp dick and the crisp sheets
the same color of these walls—as my t shirt dries to my skin
and the faintest scent of ground zero

sifts down on the walls
whiter than the wingtip vortices
of melting in the morning light.

Every city's a response to the indifference of geology.
From the pier on West Street the towers were sun on steel.

I felt the tone-hole sockets vibrate in my hand,
I felt *what does it take to win your love for me*

woozy like bourbon, insistent as the crowds pushing around me
to the lunch carts and heavenly benches.

By the time I pressed the buttons Junior Walker's sax
was swallowing the elevator.

I rose up a vertigo of keys into the plane lingo
of anodized aluminum and blue-skied-out window panes;

if the merging of writing and bureaucracy started urban life,
if a city could levitate on arbitrage and junk bonds—

if the sea above were like the Hudson down here, if
I tried, I tried, I tried in every way I could.

The vents were cooling me down
I had a check for a half million in my pocket (a lot for those days).

At the sky lobby on the 47th I looked out
at the barges and tugs on the filthy gold water—

the Colgate clock on the Jersey side ticking
in the late capitalist haze; looked out into the mica flakes of air—

the gulls flat as floating money,
the sun spilling on a geology of invisible numbers.

WARHOL / BLUE JACKIE

Her face catches you as you come around the corner
and see her on the far wall,

in the white silence after the docents and guards
have left you there alone

(behind the veil the interior is chaos, the Lincoln slows down,
the roses slide onto the pink dress),

she comes to you—a kitsch Mona Lisa
bella donna of the roses, face of revision.

After the black-light has gone over the mesh,
and the negative has burned itself out—

the broad planes of her cheeks, the almond eyes
glazed with valium, the numbed-out mouth

(is this just complicity with the media
or the transaesthetic fetish of a nation?)

the impossible presence, the veil almost wrapping
her face spreading the pixilation.

WORLD TRADE CENTER / MAIL RUNNER / '73

There was no languor, no drowsy trade winds,
or stoned-out stupor of lapping waves,

only news, the big board of crime,
corporate raiding, selling short and long.

It didn't matter, I was no Ishmael.
I just hovered there in the thick of the material—

at the edge of a skyline of money,
rising in a glass box.

It was comic to think Bachelard believed elevators
had destroyed the heroism of stair-climbing.

In the rush of soaring metallic, past the whiff of 4-martini lunches,
up gearless traction in transparency,

waves of cool air coming from the vents.
At the 85th in a sky lobby we stalled out and the sun

flooded the glass / the river / the cliffs.
Jersey was just gouache and platinum coming apart—
a glistening smudge

and some nagging line from Roethke I'd been reading—
circulating the air:
"It will come again. Be Still. Wait."

WARHOL / ELECTRIC CHAIR / '63

The red spreads like Christmas wrapping—
the green, a field in a Caucasian rug.

It's almost beautiful without the metal plates for the head
(though the plug on the floor is visible).

Before decorator colors & Hockney,
Calvin Klein in the summery Hamptons,

before there were—switches to break the flow

my mother used to say never touch a radio when you're in the bathtub,
never fly a kite near transmission lines.

But still, it's furniture
still, it's a typical American way to go—

it's Sing Sing, the silhouette of Ethel Rosenberg.

In the rheostatic air, the absent man heard "She Loves You,"
the British invasion and the flat line arrived at once.

Outside Negroes were eaten by dogs.
Johnson was sworn in. Cuba turned red in the green sea.

WORLD TRADE CENTER / BLACK HOLES / '74

I may have flunked physics
but I was full of black holes
and wind that was slamming the tower

as I rose in the glass box
up to the 80th with a check
from Chilean Line. Black holes

opened relativity, created frozen stars.
In the sky lobby on the 99th I loafed
over headlines of John Dean's testimony

and the suicide of a CEO—
I heard the relativity of the wind.
Everything was like. I was trapped in similes

I hated. I couldn't leave my head
and so the sound was insidious, then beautiful,
Then . . . it was there

(if I say I once heard bird-bone pipes
in an old church in the Caucasus
like this wind blowing in the tracery

of the top floors, in the pipelines
and farther up). Through the glass
I could see the other tower wavering—

the silver like broken mica—
I was falling matter dislodged by the idea
of a place from which nothing can return:

Jackie Wilson's tremolo, Paganini's
broken wires, the frantic shaking
of the small bells at the altar

going up into some place
beyond the smudged-out sky
above the radar needle,

above the planes coming out
of the fog on their way to Newark.

It was possible to hoist an object
out of a black hole with a rope—
this bit of knowledge I was hanging on to.

WARHOL / RACE RIOT / '63

We were watching the Yankees in black & white on a Magnavox,
while across county, or state, there was a billy-club,
a German Shepherd and the white line unraveled on the road.

I remember Hector Lopez's stance, because it gave me a spasmodic feel,
like what I would later learn in salsa and mamba,
and even on the screen we could see a white line.

On the other side of the county or the state,
black faces were arrested in Liquitex, dissolved by chemicals
so the trace of sweet flowers or burning rubber almost disappeared.

I was watching a relief pitcher named Arroyo, how carefully he went
to the rosin bag, how the white powder dusted his hand, and then
I poured a Coke where now there's just pixilation and red wash.

The couch was new leather; the lawns on the block
undulated like outfields into the evening
where the sun flattened in the emulsified sky.

ELEVATOR, MIDTOWN, '74

We were falling, just after sunrise and metallic
coffee into Nietzsche's cracked-open head.
The black shaft swallowing the red ass of the sun.

We lived between our zipless love
and the global village, law and order rained
down on us like Lichtenstein's yellow dots,
the gearless traction was Monk *Off Minor*.

I saw the rising sun on the glass,
the fat Oldsmobiles going up in flames,
my face disappearing in your rear-view mirror
after we spent all night solving what we couldn't—

Monk's keys were leaving the wires,
traction, whine, thin-out, disappear—
before the door opened and the day began.

Two

A-TRAIN / ZIGGURAT / ELEGY

I.

The tender head of the he-goat (on the cover)
stares through the branches of a golden tree,

and I'm just moving on a system of fuses,
while the fruit stands of Spanish Harlem fly above,

and even now remembering when we were here
after Nixon waved goodbye and rose in the chopper.

Even now seeing it through the double glass
as *Ur of the Chaldees* (revised and updated)

Sir Leonard Woolley's Excavations at Ur
flares on the yellow cover in the momentary dark

that wrapped our bodies, all night like violent paint
on the sheets; like the broken fire escape of our building.

At 125th, the guy next to me reading *Another Country*;
the white guy passed out in a suit and a brown bag.

The steel screeches the tracks, and the vaults light up.

2.

To Woolley, the Crash and Wall Street
were a Fata Morgana of palms shattered in ice.

He paid baksheesh to the locals and they kept digging—
baked clay and gypsum;

Woolley loved cow dung, mud plaster huts: the world from bottom up.

"We found a clay figurine of a pig,
spindle-whorls of baked clay prove that thread was spun here."

———

In the last days of Babylon
a mathematician gave zero a name,
not far from where Woolley dug.

No great thing comes without a curse, said Sophocles—
So Zero = hollow circle = cylinder seal—
"Skulls and seeds and all good things are round" (Nabokov).

3.

You made his lines, which were opaque as ashes,
seem clear as our confusion.

("the diagonal black's a broken body")

it was after the show, we walked from Tung-Lai Shun
to the Bowery to the Bridge and back.

"I like bridges," Franz Kline said, "if people want to see bridges
in my lines that's good."

And when we fell into the shadow of the morning,
why did we stop talking, after all, after all of it, after everything.

You disappeared on the train reading Merleau-Ponty
I got lost in Queens on the E.

4.

I ran mail a whole summer down Greenwich and West.
Before it even started, before we roamed Radio Row
for 78s of Ellington and the Blanton Trio,

before the yin-yang of real estate
under the Kensett skies over the river,
the wrecking balls took Radio Row down:

florists, groceries, record shops, restaurants
the whole mid-century slid into a pit
and the sun made gothic trees of the falling windows.

Out of *res ipsa loquitur*
Out of Port Authority and Chase,
Rockefeller and Tobin,
the Twin Towers rose from the garbage.

5.

But to Woolley it wasn't Iraq, it wasn't post-empire or Faisal's kingdom,
it was precise and chaotic digging into the beginning,
as if the piece of the snake's tail that was swallowed by the mouth
made the full-circle of history.

"All the bodies lay on their backs, rigidly extended: hands crossed below the
    stomach
the graves, dug into the silt were"

—after the flood: decayed brick, ashes,
potsherds, flints, clay figurines—

I used to think of post-diluvian as theoretical.
But if you ask: what became of the Sumerians?

"It grieves me to watch the end of any good work
to which men have given so much thought and skill."

Woolley might have agreed with Duchamp,
who thought America's greatest art was its plumbing
and NYC the summation of sewage pipes and sinks,

which join here in the 59th Street Station
where we're stuck, and before the lights go out I can see
the pale blue and white tiles glistening like Lucca della Robbias.

6.

I watched it half-drugged by the sun off the West Street pier:

"First, there was the construction of the core or rectangular elevator-service
area where all the interior columns were clustered together. From the core,
the floor system reached in a clear and unobstructed clean sweep to the
exterior wall. . . . Although few tenants subsequently took full advantage of
the dramatic interior layout potential, the fact remains that the architecture
offered great possibilities. It was at the core that the giant kangaroo cranes
lifted the steel from the outside."

7.

We met on a cold morning
when the women were gathering dew.
START AGAIN: We met at a party in a loft on Greene St.
in the no-gravity of Barsamian's big canvasses;
post-Magritte you called it; a vagina and no head, breasts but no limbs.

The red wine was Chilean, this was after Allende and Neruda.
I watched your mouth in the dark reflection of the window
beyond which the light of the towers glared the black red.

But still the need to ask—who wrapped the day in nectar?
Who cracked the sun over the hedges?
Who saw the light flare off the towers at dusk?

What's loss if not an open grave
where the heart is eaten by worms.

8.

Woolley thought the original Ur was built on a low mound
rising only just above the surrounding swampland—

"Here all traces of human activity ceased and we were at the bottom of
    Mesopotamia."

—

Among the many things the Sumerians handed down
is the story of a flood, cf. *Gilgamesh*,

and after that, kingship was sent down from on high
so civilization could start again.

A tweed jacket and vest in the Iraqi sun, mid-winter evenings,
two martinis up, a supply from Harrods.

9.

1/30/06

"John Hendricks and the cameraman Al Diehl
were standing up in the back hatch of an Iraqi armored vehicle,
not a Humvee, something 'softer,' taping the patrol."

I was driving back to Hamilton
in snow on Rt. 17, and the words came
like distortion of sound from the dashboard.

"A combined operation with the Iraqi army and
coalition forces," the voice said, "soft targets."
IED jammers, wireless—embedded with the 4th Infantry.

Your students always live
in their seats, their faces smooth,
teeth shining, John '83, bristling

rugby-energy in his chair.
"John was bleeding from the head,"
Am I alive? Don't tell Ann.

10.

And when I think of I / then we / then back to I—
in that spot where before I knew you, I watched the ditch dug:
the mist and silt on my arms
running past the hulls of Cunard and Chilean.

"From within this 'bathtub excavation' came the detritus of early European
settlement, for this part of the Hudson was first used as a garbage dump
and then filled in to extend the island westward.

Burned and capsized vessels and anchors
clay pipes, hand-blown bottles—drinking glasses, salt-glaze pots; shoes;
bones of countless animals, cannon balls, a litho of Grover Cleveland."

11.

We kept going around and around and at the zero spot
the hole became a black hole in which you,
you had to confess your past, and so there it was,

was again; the marsh reeds were high and we were in them
in the lemony light as the trucks on the Pike drilled past us.

And now the lights out; the car steaming with bodies,
the stink of the bourbon and cigarettes of the guy passed out next to me.
A silver flash on the facing track, then dark.

12.

9/21/03

All day the campus floated in light,
the pond bronze with carp

not mud-brown late-March clotted debris—
but darting, transparent, cutting past

a large gold or walleye; trees
of riotous color left late summer in the curb.

The granite stone of Lawrence Hall
glittered through the elms,

and lawn rolled as we walked
down-slope to the rugby field,

close to where Ann was chasing the twins as
they tumbled down the hill.

You had returned with clips
of the Al Qaeda camp in Pakistan

where you lived for weeks
among the poor and angry.

"Death to America" on school walls.
Poppy head and gladiator. White Satan.

The war had just started
as you returned to the City

to your new job as the anchor.
But the images called you back.

Camouflage of the embedded—
the Humvee tracks, acronyms for Iraq.

13.

Yamasaki made it to withstand the crash of a 747,
the vortex, the phantom, the lateral-winds,

exterior walls carrying the vertical loads and wind

and they came: exterior columns from Seattle,
beams from Alabama, trusses from Texas, columns from Pittsburgh, floor
    assemblies from Newark

PONYA WTC 213.00 236B4-9 558 35 TONS

Under the cranes, hydraulic lifts, guy wires, derricks
I sat with a couple Sabretts and a Coke,

the ozone blotting out Jersey.

The flood left silt and minerals
which Woolley's men sifted like black flour.

And then it came
("Only the Gods can live forever"),

and Gilgamesh was left to wander the skin of the earth,
friendless, looking for God.

It swallowed everything,
though sky and water are still emblems of the possible,

alluvium, crushed fish bones, pummeled rocks.

———

O house of heaven rising
O foundation of earth
O elemental zig zag

City of the moon god Nanna,
home of Abraham; wind-bitten, badlands of the soul;
water-marked buttes, blades of hawk wings of the body.

Today it's Tell al-Muqayyar where
Agatha Christie (who spent time with Woolley) set *Murder in Mesopotamia*.

You forget that Nebuchadnezzar inherited the region a millennium later.

You forget because it's just an excavation now.
like my mind when it blanks into itself,

like the horizon when it goes black and the flame
of one oil refinery flickers out at the Syrian border

where once I picked Armenian bones out of the dirt.

15.

We held out for Valentine and Virgin Mary.
In cold hard light. Worm Moon and no sap in trees,
there was blood on our sheets.

The pipes were frozen.
Chinese kites stuck on wires.

We painted each other in the I-love-you dyes of
expectation and faith,

each red letter stamped *jagad-a-krese*:
in Armenian: written on your forehead:

fate—Armenian nuance:
it's on you, others see it—you don't.

In the end I couldn't come through for you,

and the end was the beginning of late February:
entitled, luscious, leap-year.

Here's to life. *Genat-sut.*
Here's to March, Mars,
God who protects the land.

16.

3/1/06

The email came like a blink on the screen after midnight.
I was up emailing friends in Beirut who were describing
the twisted steel that was rusting in the markets.

"This is like being in a circle of Dante's *Inferno*,"
Ann wrote, "We're here at the VA hospital.
John has the best doctors possible.

He's speaking now, though in several languages,
Chinese, French, sounds that come pell mell.

The children are doing ok. Talking with their father;
everyone is holding together.
The support of so many gives us great strength."

17.

Etemenanki
tower of hands and dead bodies

: Babel / *Babuli*: gate to God

chthonic, zig zag of hubris
(not far from Ur),

Prometheus revisited:
does God have a right to heaven alone?

———

Pieter Brueghel had it all wrong:
there was solid masonry in the middle,
a winding path circling the eight towers,
baked brick glued with asphalt

only to have the builders
wake up: confused or confounded (*balal* / Heb.)
as in a writer full of puns
a scatterer of language—

Put down your tools
and walk: diasporan—meaning

polyglot mountains; lakes of continents

(in Armenian we call it *garod*: longing: sickness after exile, need for the
    beloved).

18.

I follow the cochineal thread of the skyline,
a single weft pulled by a crow's beak
over the high-rises of Edgewater.

19.

Days I sank in the rubble, and the noise
drove out of my head the most basic words

like now when we're mute and
the wheels of the train drown out the noise in my head.

Below the B-2 level
the multi-million line Nynex switching station

generator / air-conditioning / giant computer—
was filling up the hole left by the garbage of history.

I couldn't imagine a silicon brain
or hear the humming of the inaudible frequencies

of magnetic core memory
of the integrated circuits of a capacitor—

some days I found places along the pier
where I sat and went blank

(this was before Ginsberg
introduced me to meditation),

staring at the tugs pushing the freight barges
toward Staten Island till red merged with black

and the black became a point of no return
like you fading out of sight on the pier,

20.

and black hole of loneliness rose up in me.

And now the shaking train starts to pull out of Columbus Station.

"Omens," said Ovid, "are wont to wait upon beginnings."

You said:

32

Poets are paranoid, apocalyptic

style-drunk, sense-lusters, hypochondriacs.

21.

The creosote vaults at 42nd
covered in day-glo neon Pollack
over the girders of "peace but fuck you anyway"

the guy reading Baldwin getting out;
the drunk could be dead against
the window scratched: *Fallujah*.

22.

On the street I heard that the Indians
were like cold-blooded dancers at high altitudes.

Mohawks who had come down from Canada.

I watched them glide with hot rivets
and cold steel into the azure of near oblivion.

Some days they disappeared in light
as if the narrow beams of air came undone

and they floated between steel and blue
like lost angels of the Carracci.

My head spiraled from the fumes of coffee and
yellow bulls, red cranes, green trucks, pale blue drilling rigs

bull's liver; gooseneck; clam shell; orange peels;
192,000 tons of steel—

23.

I was beginning to see Woolley: after the inexorable, rotting earth began
to sink into itself, after the metal and the bones disappeared.

After the Treaty divvied up the Arab world
and the latitudes were lubricious,

spilling over Basra where J. E. Taylor found
his mound of pitch and inscriptions of the nameless ruin.

Ubaid, Uruk, Jamdat Nasr—
the weeds—scribes and skeletons.

24.

Just before the lights went black
the silver-Pullman-flash of another train

with the flag on every car now,
glowing before it goes dark again
somewhere past 23rd.

25.

I loved your love of myth and ritual.
I loved reading Eliade with you on the train.

The uroboric windows hugged the car
the spring rain washed away the serpent's tail.

Just as our moment passed like Ash Wednesday

when you returned with the sign on your head.
Everything went black and silent

like that Saturday when Jesus lay in the tomb
before the apotheosis we waited for all spring long.

I loved how you took me down Pentecostal
without restraint or faith

into the dark vaults lower than the 4th St. station.
No mythological bullshit here

you were the realest of the real
with your mad black hair and your crushing childhood.

Your lips of plum and turpentine
were signifier and signified,

the crêpe de Chine, the lace, the chinoiserie,
the strange clock your father brought from Thrace

kept ticking at us as if we were in Attica.

26.

2/15/06

Some days I heard John's voice in my head in
the presumptuous way a poem wants to enter the other

for a glimpse of the unutterable
and from the fragments in Ann's email:

like headlights in fog
floating down the well

the Blackhawk chopping sand-wind

the tank-grate-metal-hit

the snake crawls along the jaw
then out the hole of the back.

27.

It was true: the Armenians got to Jesus first
at least officially, ahead of Rome,

and this devastated you because you had
believed all those truths of catechism

all that dogma which spelled backwards
is humiliation and extravagance

the kind of thing Fellini made you see
in *Roma* and we left the Angelica laughing

at your confirmation dress and your mother's
anxious rosary you carried in your purse.

28.

Who is the other who
floats between what you see

and what is there:
think of the other going silent,

screen fuzz smoke,
hours away on TV.

Came as dumb smoke

into my house.
The jade plant leaves,

tongue of the cat,
pan on the stove,

the cardamom and clove
moved in their currents.

Outside the sky was searing blue
honeysuckle wafting through.

There was nowhere to go.
Sat down. Got up.

Stared at the iBook.
Walked around.

No phone service.
The cell's dead too.

29.

"Dalí once told me my work was related to John of the Cross.
I've never read him," Kline said, "I wouldn't know."

You thought melting clocks was a cheap gimmick
like most of surrealism

and Dalí: hyper, overwrought, esthete,
but Kline caught Dr. J and Nijinsky in a stroke;

he saw the truth about us in diagonal slashes.

30.

Days I was almost fired; checks late to the bank;
mail in piles by the meter machine. The grillages transfixed us:

twenty-eight grillages supporting the columns of the elevator core of the
    North Tower,
core box-shaped columns and box beam framing.
Who had ever heard of anything like this?

A gang of workers guided the grillage onto the concrete slab or footing
seventy feet below street level, foundation to erection, each one:
thirty-four tons, fifteen feet long, eleven feet wide, and seven feet high.

"Domenico Delicarpini, a thirty-year-old, $140-a-week laborer, married
and the father of four children"—plunged thirty feet on May 15, 1969, when
some planking gave way. Fractured his neck and spinal cord, will never work
again; awarded $500,000 by the State Supreme Court in Bronx in a case
against the Port Authority and Tishman.

31.

The drum roll of wheels over tracks—
my head synced with the streak

of Euclid Ave. Blue C
8th Ave. Local World Trade Center (still up)

against the black and white ticking of the tiles
dissolving into neon dust and I asked

32.

where were we going as the rhododendrons fell into themselves
and the park seemed to levitate on the fume.

Peachwood strips will drive out evil spirits.
We drove the brown Corolla to Rhinebeck for the weekend.

The ash and spruce were resinous in our throats;
you set out pots of sedum, dumb-cakes, dreaming bannocks,

at high noon you broke an egg in a bowl
and read the fantastic shapes of the flowing whites.

We lit our fire of bones; baun = beacon,
bane fire for banishing evil.

Screw all things civic and patriotic
you wrote in big letters on a note pad

after seeing Agnew's plastic face
rise like a balloon on the screen.

Stonehenge and Tiahuanaco.
Bloom watching Gerty McDowell

as the roman candles poured their fire.
Read it to me again.

33.

The first incoming message arrived over a direct
teleprinter circuit, a confirmation of a sale of spice

from Ceylon to Colombia, 9:54 AM
EST Tuesday, December 15, 1970
tenth and eleventh floors of the North Tower.

Mornings I lived on gravity, wind, and fear.
The observation elevators, sky lobbies,
glass-sides ran faster than a subway,

and the glass wrapped me
as I looked back at myself
as in a fun-house room where

each plane shattered
any idea of the whole
though the parts were more than the sum

—the way the style
of the sundial projects the shadow,
the way sunyata knows all entities

are empty. Was this why
the Mayan symbol for zero
was a tattooed man in a necklace

with his head thrown back?

———

I watched the pioneer firms
unload into the unfinished space;
the Hudson sun poured down the core.

On the street it was Christmas
the scotch was pouring at the White Horse
the homeless guys in boxes

stretched out on visible corners
in empty lots and church porticos.

It was hardly Thoreau's open-air house
but it was a strange brew of wind and light
clanging metal and teleprinter circuits.

At the topping-out ceremony on the 23rd
the iron workers soldered a flag
to a thirty-six-foot long, four-ton column

hoisted by a kangaroo crane
and then it came—
a thirty-foot Christmas tree

on a three-story-high exterior wall section
on the southeast corner of the building.
The regulation was three cans of beer per guest.

34.

the train screeches into the dark
the bodies' frottage heating the in-breath

stuck below the Village

35.

for the underworld God they harvested grain
the naked ground at 120°
the same color as Kline's white.

"The Ziggurat is a peculiar feature of Mesopotamian architecture . . .
it is still not certain whether the ziggurats of the Ur III period were the
expressions of a new religious concept or where such buildings raised by
Ur-Nammu in various of his cities were merely the final stage
of a long architectural development."

36.

Franz Kline—

black bites back—takes the head off
the illusion so that white is

not the empty face, the apparition,
but the joyful stone, the sheet of Jesus.

Not the lost man in Lapland,
the white sea, the buffalo robe,

but the belly of any fish—
the canvas gaze,

whatever opalescent film
the oyster brings to surface.

37.

Between *Bananas* and *Annie Hall*
there was a big hole in the window

south of Coentis Slip, south of Warhol
where we walked our thousand miles

 never jumping from the plank.
"Ford to City: Drop Dead"

was the stuffed insulation
in our half-done loft south of Franklin,

where we heard the hidden fifths of Philip Glass
rise like isotopic rings up the shaft

of the invisible elevator we rode
into the ecstatic, garbage-filled glow

of purple-red as it lit up
the McAllister tugs

and the barely visible birds
that followed in the Ferry.

38.

Everything was tangled up in blue.
Seeping glaze on the Delft jug,

liquefaction of the Virgin's silk
as it spread in Titian's cobalt

to a fleshy embrace and the green meadows
in the distance fade to hammered light.

Light we pulled into a string of glass
that seeped out of the long vibration

of Miles's *Blue in Green*
like slow time in the empty lot

after soot and rain and rush,
the Ferry out of sight,

my bones electric with the hum
of the cable of the Bridge at 3 AM

and the dying lights of the Bowery.
Bill Evans making the rain thin

to a beam of haze before the
horn comes back from under water.

39.

When the lights came back
the white Pumas on the ad strip flashed

onto my page—*Joda Por Una* Bud Light
glared under the white *Osama* slashed.

40.

We could have gone together
beads of carnelian, lapis, glazed fruit, gold.

The look in the mirror sent me away.
The ruins of houses and the cemetery.

When is it ever the right time?
Plano-convex brick in our archeological jargon—

Why did Apollo give the car to Phaethon?
Layers of debris from burnt buildings covered from red to sooty black—

It was a hell of a fire.
Lumps of clay plastered over the stoppers of store-jars—

Will the end come like this?
Seal impressions found in the rubbish strata with the tablets.

41.

The black comes down on us.
The Inuit understood this.
They fished in total darkness.

All December sky and water
converged and they learned to catch by feel.
There was fire light and they loved in it.

42.

Flaring new gingko leaves,
islands of tulips smearing by us

(O strongest you in the hour of danger, in crisis! O truer than steel!)

and we get out here under the deafening chopper NYPD
the sky brilliant as the yellow cab

How your soft opera-music changed . . .

we can't hear each other; in the deafening silence
"the poem becomes desperate conversation" (Celan)

Sleepless amid her ships, her houses, her incalculable wealth

your father remembered
the pilots falling from the white heat o of the Japanese sun

the chrysanthemum singeing into smoke rings on the postage stamps
stuffed in his bomber jacket.

O superb! O Manhattan

the stretcher disappeared into the chopper,
into the world-blur of flags around the UN.

43.

Even if we met at junctures elegiac (Hart Crane). RE-DO.
Even if the windows opened to techno trance not far from where Val Solanis
    shot Warhol
as the strobes faded out; even if we lived in the cold water flat
of embracing pronouns and the train shook the lath and the mirrors

I was sitting all day looking out

44.

I would sing now on that lyre
decomposed but for the brilliant golden
head of the he-goat and the braided

lapis beard carved so finely
you can feel the roots
and the spiral braids come alive

in your hand just as now the sound
of those strings in the half-life of the carbon
purrs in the isotopic air

of those hecatombs where Woolley's black light
scanned a silver tumbler, fluted and chased,
in some color that's gone,

45.

as the rings
unspool out of the whiteness
that hovers on the canopy

of the higher buildings
of lower Broadway over the
underpass to the Holland tunnel

as the trace of my passing
leaves the phosphor

of some thought that twines
the air as the body thins

and day comes
with its faint industrial orange
glow and sun on river.

Three

THREE DECADES

Pol Pot called 1975 the year zero of his reign—
the year he would purify his enemies—

the year we followed Gerald Ford
into the U-haul of the GOP

that year I dreamed of green wind & auroras & falling orchids
& the dissolution of OPEC

as it floated off the black wave of the Persian Gulf.

———

On a terrace on Greene St.
in July '75 I could see the pylons of the World Trade towers
through the cracks of buildings

half-drunk on a chaise . . . looking up at the sky of smog and milky way
the pin pricks of light filtering down on the chiasmic streets—

& it floated down—*cyclonic zero of the word*—
a bitten-off, hyper Lowell-phrase
of winter in this city when the steel of things wrapped the air,

floated down and down.
a permutation of a political moment—a pure clear word—of 1953

as Ike's ascension seemed to signify something old, something new;
as one good liberal put it, "if we wanted a bald golfer in the White House
we could have elected Ben Hogan."

———

It came back to me . . . December
on the ice at Rockefeller Center

when I first saw my face floating on the cold smooth surface
beneath the splintering glass-color of the giant tree
and the faces plastered to the glass of the shops and restaurants.

I floated in the December air into the absence of the new era
as Kennedy's death began to sink into the nation.

At night when my parents were asleep
I flicked the dial to find half the stations snowy
or the picture slipping beneath the horizontal band,

the faces of Oswald & Ruby faded into
the whiteness of news lights and tabloid pages.

READING DICKINSON / SUMMER '68

In the hermetic almost dark
under the fluorescent dizz

I found her broken nerves,
smoke coming off the dashes,
the caps like jolts to the neck,

the pried-open spaces between vowels
where the teeth bit off twine
and the tongue was raw then cool with ice.

The air of the stockroom after lunch
was the marbleized silence of the
small blank pages she stitched into privacy.

Air of paper and faint glue
bond, carbon, graph, yellow pads,

in the stockroom I could read alone—
the confetti of money dissolved on the blank wall.

After work, I slid the numbered poems
on blue mimeo into my playbook,
and felt the open field

the zig-zagging past cornerbacks,
the white lines skewed to heaven.

Excuse my mood—unbridled, chemical,
her scrawled messages smooth to the mind,

excuse my absence, again and yes, then, too—

the cold stone of the Palisades was there
after we split—

alone naked in the Hudson,
the water greasing me in the tepid, chemical mix,

before I returned
to the cement of 9w in my father's Skylark

the night black and soundless within.

GRANT'S TOMB

I.

All we had done was lick a square of anonymous paper
and the elevators disappeared into the metal grates

on top of Carmen Hall where we saw
Lincoln's face in the cloud-bank that passed,

2.

by dark we had walked into the seventh house under
the sign of pouring water, under Jupiter and Mars
along a flank of the Drive by the river.

Between the seen and the unseen we followed
the halos on the cars and hydrants and your cigarette
glowed like a headlight.

Out of the restless clouds,
the high-rises on the Jersey side—green, acid-red,
vitreous purple, were lava lamps out of focus,

the Doric columns shook,
a dome rose out of the trees
the crypts of Appomattox sank into the Hudson.

3.

We believed in *Love's Body*,
between the outstretched hands of Jesus
and Janis Joplin's slumped torso,

we were in the flow of vessels to the soul
and back to the body like a beltway around a city
any city, as long as it served the doors,

which brought the clear void to Nixon's chemical war.

4.

The last time we saw Sopolla, half-padded
clowning in the locker room, soft, round-faced
eager, immovable tackle, coach's dream.

We waded into the flash-lit dark. The sprinklers
wet us down, the lawns loved our naked legs,
the pool was blue light all night.

None of us could say Qaung Ngai.
No one could say, Kool-Aid, dog-tag, poncho;
No one could breathe green tea, joy-ride, black flag.

5.

As if the Civil War ended here
where Riverside Drive pushed to Harlem
and the Black voices of the choir spilled into the river,

where James Baldwin swept the pages
from his father's pulpit into piles of trash
that wound along the sides of the tomb.

"Take me to your leader. Take me to your heart"—
the black spray paint floated in the dark
on the marble columns—

6.

We lived in Nixon's demonology between
Joe Namath and Andy Warhol—
the hard targets beneath the canopy.

Cambodia was glowing phosphor. Our bodies
were torqued like the stone eagles at the entrance to the tomb.

We weren't afraid of pain or death
or the granite of history, we knew better,
we kept saying we knew, we had apprehension,

we got air waves from radio Hanoi
heard violins, Buddhist chants,
the sounds of Cobras and F-45s

enemy movement. Sopolla
was jungle juice, wires gone wrong.

7.

What did we know of the green floating scum of the Yazoo,
or his vision of wasted Yankees on the Chickasaw Bluffs,
before Vicksburg went down and the Union was possible.

He was always calm, always dissembling, always chain-smoking
cigars, walking over corpses and cartridge boxes
mud and horse-knees. And now we knew it,

we who believed gray matter, spine, and semen
were one; we believed we were bees and ants
walking into the absolute darkness of the chamber.

8.

In the come-down at dawn
beneath the fulgurating sycamores
and the crocuses burning into crayons

there was no morning-creation
just Nixon's valium face on the screen,
bronze, scaled, flushed,

and the esoteric barges moving on the river.
We sat on the granite steps
beneath the fan-winged eagles,

the air was green, the mausoleum
shimmered in purple haze.

SELF-PORTRAIT WITH BIRD

I remember cutting out of school for the amusement park in Palisades,
the terror of speed as the cars spilled down the rollercoaster's gutted tracks,
before I walked to a spice market in the next town where the Syrian grocer
gave me a bag of sumac and told me to catch a jackdaw.

What was a jackdaw but a word that stuck in my ear and so I began looking
for a dazzling colored bird, and only now remembering this, as I'm stuck in
a sky lobby of a midtown building looking across the river at the light thick
as glue on the Palisades. I can see the electrified claw of steel wrapping
the Turnpike where every exit opens into black sounds.

It's an ordinary morning, the coffee bitter and tinny, the sun cochineal
on the bridge, the horizon bituminous glass and a bird cutting through—
like something out of Calder, and I can even see the heads
of angels on the backboards of the courts on Lenox Avenue.

What did I know of a jackdaw then, a simple gray-black bird
that's flying in this late sky between the cables of the GW
swallowing the cochineal the horizon pulls away.

THE ALLEY

In the alley of broken glass, after rain,
the buildings breathed soot,

the drunks were wrapped in cardboard,
their faces obscured in yellow light.

It was early morning and I stank of the grease vat.
Aristotle said a void is a place where no one is.

All morning men were walking into the day's trade
the light skittering like silver credit cards

from the punched-out windows of the Vista Hotel.
Lazarus left the cave just as Jesus looked up.

A drunk was summoned by the sun on the chrome of a truck.
I sat on the curb waiting for the ginkgos to go up in flames.

EARLY SPRING

When I pick up the phone, there's a voice
in the perforated holes, who wouldn't say it's like surf—
far away as the Bay of Bengal.

Here, there's wind in the jackpines,
I can see cones scattered on the last patches of white,
the conicles of seed like a priest's black hood.

I can see corn stubble on the hillside fields,
muddy ruts leeching the snow, red buds
barely visible on branches that brush the window.

Out of the blue, pellets of hail pelt the red tin roof of the side porch,
then rain, smell of thaw, and the arms remember July,
before it's back to snow squalls, and the heart's a tire spinning in mud.

My daughter, just four, runs out the door (her hair
the color of Moroccan olives) before the voice comes
through the holes into the squall. Somewhere outside a city

he was born where sounds of zithers and flutes
dissolved in the streets, goats and quince spotted the fields.
The day leaves some crocuses, patches of white.

BLUE ROOM

for George Arus (1915–196?)

I.

Bread lines were dissolving on Second Ave.
Staten Island fog dulled the horns,

the lamp-lit snow trailing into cold rain
like confetti around FDR's motorcade,

but it was seamless air, tongue and slide
breaking across the partials,

more than Helen Forrest doing "Softly
as a Morning Sunrise" or Shaw's manic trilling

into the high morning where everything falls:
the swirling lights, the acid-rust of gravity

that feeds the downtown cabs running
on war bonds and lost radio waves.

The poppy-colored walls screamed,
the sweet arms and legs were light then dark.

You dropped down so many flights
you thought you were floating back up

into the dirigible clouds,
into the rain coming in trefoils off the Garden roof

into the blue room of the Hotel Pennsylvania.

2.

You could ride the impulse beyond itself
part of the essence / age-old fire /

(the Armenian past was a smear of grease
on the chassis line at the Ford plant in Detroit)

cooling into the big blow,
the invisible coming off the Hudson,

tonguing the singing thing
the way you would do *Lover* after the war

after the blonde woman left you
for the whiskey-colored rooms in a western city.

The A-train slammed the girders of Penn Station,
the floor was smooth as any track.

3.

You lived out on the edge of the golden horn
not the Dardanelles but the one you made

where the spray came off the broken edge
and the water lapped you all night long.

You traveled across the dark,
thin, and keen, and cutting

like the high D in "The Thrill Is Gone"
as the ghost notes drifted

into the other life,
that rose as smoke so you could see it

like breathing ropes of myrrh
that poured out of the chalice on the altar;

all night it rose in coils
to the ceiling of the blue room

into that last existence, that letting loose,
the turns so sweet and smooth

there was no need for embellishment.
Who can stay up there, all night long?

9/11, EMILY DICKINSON

a piece of lamp post flew onto Rector Street,
everything fell out, beams, pieces
without a color but the light.

all I saw were spinning things,
a wheel from a plane on a car,
a piece of lamp post flew onto Rector Street.

a torso-black-window-cloud,
and the cover of the book pink and worn as skin—
dare you see a Soul at the White Heat?

everyone was covering their mouths,
the words *Final Harvest* above her name
without a color but the light.

steel grates melted in the air,
spears of wheat like fine pencils on the cover,
a piece of lamp post flew onto Rector Street.

sidewalk disappeared beneath
pink fiberglass and white wings
without a color but the light—
dare you see a Soul at the White Heat?

SARAJEVO

1.

The needle of the minaret disappeared in fog
and we were walking between Hapsburg courtyards
and the detonated façade of the National Library,

the wooden scaffolding rising up the Moorish pediments,
the stripped cement and under-brick, and then
the sun came and the Coke stand burned red.

Out of nowhere a guard opened the black metal door—
his boyish face and soft goatee startled us, and you slid inside
before he could shrug as if he were breaking the rules.

The blue poured through the metal grid
on the glass dome and we were walking
where a carillon fell onto thumbed pages,

where students worked in the dry air
of glue and vellum, under the octagons
from which the light converged invariant and mosaic.

2.

Under the shanked-up arches I took a shot
of a patch of fresco and the paint flared—
a yellow star on a pink rosette:

Jewish / Muslim / Christian—and if it wasn't
one of Duccio's halos, it was drawn
a couple blocks away from where the gracious

open car of the arch duke and his wife Sophie
traveled into the shadow of the image,
and then rail-lines were cut

and the city was a shrinking river running down
the hillside where the shelling began from Mount
Trebević, late night, August 25, '92.

3.

I followed you up a half-sliced staircase
into the memory of microfilm and quaint
catalog trays on a second-floor landing propped by a plank,

and then you disappeared with your camera,
into the dark apse-space where the steam pipes
melted under molten glass and spread to the manuscripts.

4.

Back in the cool seminar rooms of the Hollywood Hotel,
at the edge of the city our conference went on

in the green din of post-Soviet comfort where
every third channel was porn and the arguments

about ethnic cleansing were spliced by
the disco-falsetto of the Bee Gees

and through the giant windows we watched
the women sun-bathing in the weeds

next to a bulldozer and a pile of rusted cans
as plastic swans of garbage flowed

in the sulfurous river where Princip
the archduke's assassin tried to drown himself.

5.

At Birkenau there were just white birch trees for a mile
before we reached the caved-in crematoria—so lush
the skeletons of chimneys and incinerated piles of brick surprised us.

Your family disappearing south of Krakow into the soft Polish countryside
by train with their kitchen spoons and sewing kits would have
been confused by the green shade, and even though Euclid

said any two points can be joined by a straight line,
what does that make the line from Budapest to Birkenau,

and where does that leave us under this dome
as order comes down in thin spindles of light into the dust-filled air
where a man stands on a ladder re-drawing a window?

6.

Had we fallen down some volute from the touristy hills
where we drank beer and looked out at the city

at the machines digging up the mud of Marshall Tito street
where no one was eating cabbage off sheet metal,

and the smell of roasting lamb was gorgeous
as it rose from the pavilions with their newly sealed windows.

7.

Down the boulevard past the tavernas
with their burnt offerings of meat,
the Haggadah of Sarajevo was breathing,

and you copied out the marginalia;

the copper and gold almost liquid,
the letters like bullet wounds on the calf-skin pages

from which the ink flew into the margins
of deliverance or extinction—

where Aaron's spear opened a chapter
the way the enjambed bullets hit the façade

after the lights went out and historical memory
was shaved to a hill of locusts on the flight out of Egypt,

8.

as the silks were blowing into the yellow wind
against the Ottoman pavilions of the Baščaršija

and then it came down on us like roof-soot:
the burning pages of black snow

the phantasmal voices of index cards
the extinct dictionaries, the tongues washed away

in the puny brown river—between margins and colophons,
the residue of Quaranic texts that left just a dusting

on the scattered silverware under the bridge,
the invisible wires of verbs in the acid-pocked sky

the burning glue and rag that rose
into the black hole over the library

over the vanquished trees where every letter
was a country lost between latitudes and an internet café.

9.

Past teenagers making out
on benches in the Jewish graveyard
just under the hill where the snipers opened fire

we shot our heretical need
to see the horror of the past
through a wide-angled lens

and the shutter speed snipped
the light that unrolled the violets
sprawling down the hill

where more Serbian kids chugged Cokes
and pumped all night with their Kalashnikovs
from the Sarajevo-Pale Road to the high ground.

10.

We heard the rhetoric of goats
as they hacked weeds and ate piles of cellophane

wrapped nougats at the feet of the women
selling scarves and candy

along the riverbank where the sky
snowed pulverized paper and phosphorous shells,

where they had breathed the ash-packed bindings—
and letters broke into wings in the black zinc dish of the sky,

where commas and dashes hooked the encrypted clouds
or reappeared outside the hyperlinks and cellular routers

returning to earth somewhere beyond the medusa
tongues of flags of foreign countries.

11.

Past the houses of no windows,
where the sound of Arabic was less than guttural,

where the refusal to hear the Other's testimony
was the distortion of a broken CD on a megaphone in a town square,

where the brandy bottles and spent shells
littered the picked-clean kiosk and the trace was washed away.

When we came down from the hills of Porticari
through swaths of fog and ruined houses

you said: *we found no Other, just the extension of self in the scratch marks
on the photos of the disappeared.*

12.

The sculpted slabs of tombstones
were sinking in the mud, there
where the Book of Splendor opened

between the smack of bullets
and the caved-in mikvah
where the embroidered shawls

and the gold-embossed prayer-books
sank into ruts and the violets went red
like our eyes in the photo

beneath the light that untied the Hasidic knots
in which the soul had Houdinied out
into the wild air after the expulsion from Spain.

13.

You asked: *If there is no one to listen to the story, what's left?*
The blown-out ceiling with its tinge of Duccio-color?

where we walked in and looked up
at the strange blue coming down through the triangles and octagons,

onto the plaster-dusted marble floor.

De-facing the Other is a response to the transparency of the event
look at the photos of the missing.

Books disappear like people, no tombs, the pages stink and then they're soot,
and then the air is clean again.

14.

The river was clogged with the dialectic of garbage
as we watched pages disappear on the rock-barges

that faded in the hammered gold light
that sank to bronze before its aubergine

blotted out the hills, and we let the letters
go, the focus frozen on imagining the intractable.

The restaurant was grilling chops and sausage,
the cabbage sweet, yoghurt smashed with garlic,
Croatian wine dry and cold. The streets still buzzing.

NOTES

"Warhol / Blue Jackie": "Transaesthetic fetish" from Baudrillard.

"World Trade Center / Mail Runner / '73": For Michael Hollander.

"Warhol / Race Riot / '63": For Bill Worth.

"A-Train / Ziggurat / Elegy": The following sources have been helpful, and
several quoted passages are self-evident: *Ur "of the Chaldees": A Revised
and Updated Edition of Sir Leonard Woolley's "Excavations at Ur,"* by
P. R. S. Moorey; Angus K. Gillespie's *Twin Towers: The Life of New York
City's World Trade Center*; Eric Darton's *Divided We Stand: A Biography
of New York's World Trade Center.*
Section 42: Italicized lines are from Whitman's "Drum-Taps: First O Songs
for a Prelude."

"Grant's Tomb": For Ed Harris.

"The Alley": For Doris Varjabedian Cross.

"Blue Room": George Arus (née Aroosian), my mother's cousin, was first
trombonist for Artie Shaw's band in the late 1930s and trombonist for
Tommy Dorsey's band in the 1940s.

"9 / 11, Emily Dickinson": For Chuck Strozier.
Italicized lines are from Dickinson's poem 365.

"Sarajevo": Section 11, lines 6–7, and section 13, lines 6–7 owe to Donna-Lee
Frieze's "The Face of Genocide," in *Evoking Genocide.*